baby SHARKS

KIM THOMPSON

CREATIVE EDUCATION • CREATIVE PAPERBACKS

CONT

ENTS

I Am a Pup 

On My Own 

Ocean Swimmer 

Attack! 

Speak and Listen 

Shark Words 

Reading Corner 

Index 

I AM A PUP.

I am a baby shark.

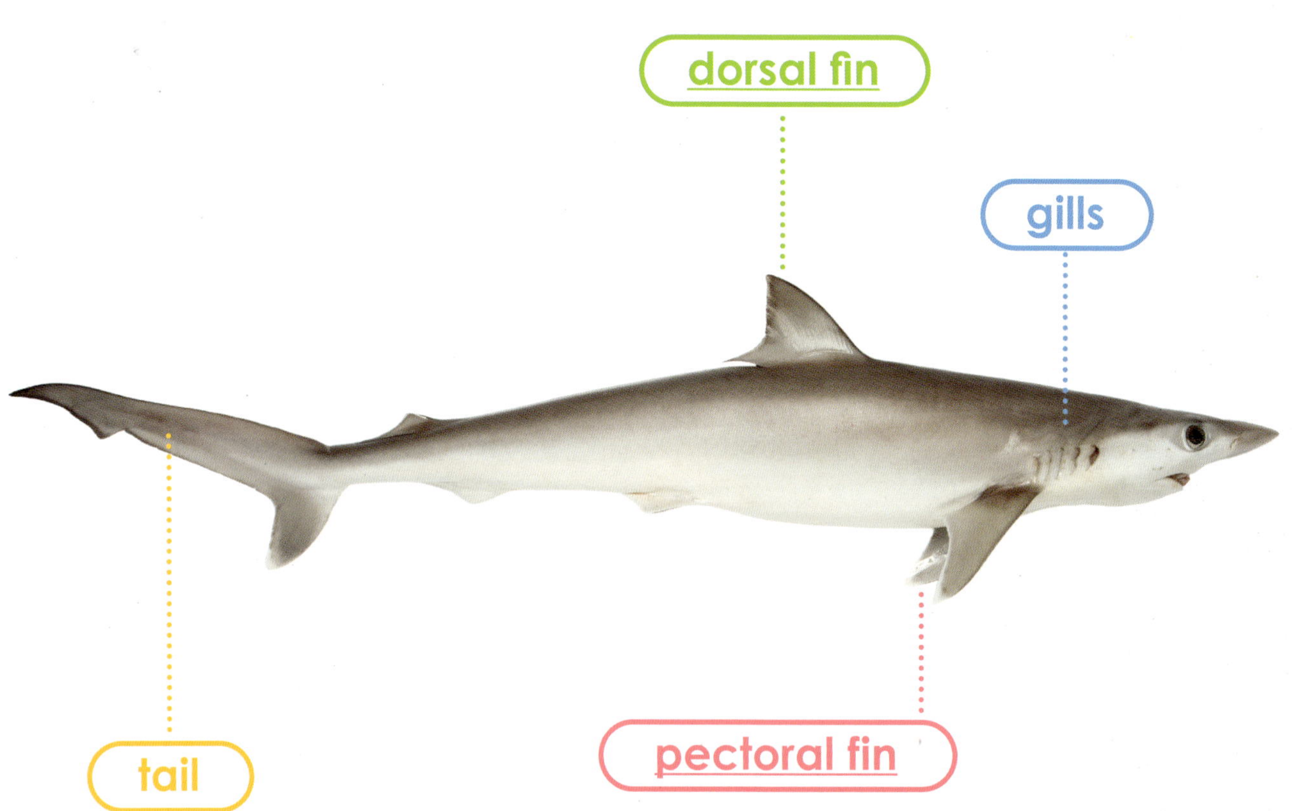

I have a great sense of smell.

I am a fish, but I did not come from an egg. My mom gave birth to a brood of live pups.

My mom does not take care of me. I could swim and hunt as soon as I was born.

My life began in warm, shallow water. As I grow, I go farther into the ocean. I eat larger prey.

I keep swimming so I do not sink.

I can swim as fast as a car!

I swim in a circle under fish, turtles, and squid. I attack from below.

My sharp teeth will grow for my whole life.

SPEAK AND LISTEN

Sharks make no sounds.

They do not have body parts that make noises.

They are silent hunters.

SHARK WORDS

brood: a group of sharks born at the same time; mako sharks have 4 to 16 pups in a brood

dorsal fin: a flap-like body part on a shark's back that helps it balance and swim in a straight line

pectoral fin: a flap-like body part on a shark's side that helps it steer through the water

prey: animals that are hunted and eaten by other animals

READING CORNER

Holub, Joan. *I Am the Shark*. New York: Crown Books for Young Readers, 2021.

McDonald, Jill. *Exploring Sharks (Hello, World! Kids' Guides)*. New York: Doubleday Books for Young Readers, 2022.

National Geographic Kids. *Five-Minute Shark Stories*. Washington, D.C.: National Geographic Kids, 2023.

INDEX

attack 11
fins 4
hunt 7, 11
mom 6, 7
ocean 8
prey 8, 11
smell.................. 5
speed................ 10
swim 7–11
teeth 11

PUBLISHED BY CREATIVE EDUCATION AND CREATIVE PAPERBACKS
P.O. Box 227, Mankato, Minnesota 56002
Creative Education and Creative Paperbacks are imprints of The Creative Company
www.thecreativecompany.us

LIBRARY OF CONGRESS CATALOGING-IN-PUBLICATION DATA
Names: Thompson, Kim, 1970- author
Title: Baby sharks / Kim Thompson.
Description: Mankato, Minnesota : Creative Education and Creative Paperbacks, [2026] | Series: Starting out | Includes bibliographical references and index. | Audience term: juvenile | Audience: Ages 4-7 Creative Education and Creative Paperbacks | Audience: Grades K-1 Creative Education and Creative Paperbacks | Summary: "Introduce beginning readers to the world of baby sharks with this life science starter. Includes photos, a labeled animal diagram, "Make a Noise" section, glossary, and further resources"-- Provided by publisher.
Identifiers: LCCN 2024043257 (print) | LCCN 2024043258 (ebook) | ISBN 9798889897545 library binding | ISBN 9781682778401 paperback | ISBN 9798889897675 ebook
Subjects: LCSH: Sharks--Infancy--Juvenile literature
Classification: LCC QL638.9 .T4867 2026 (print) | LCC QL638.9 (ebook) | DDC 597.3--dc23/eng/20250103
LC record available at https://lccn.loc.gov/2024043257
LC ebook record available at https://lccn.loc.gov/2024043258

DESIGN AND PRODUCTION
Design by Rhea Magaro
Production by Beeline Media and Design, Inc.
Art direction by Tom Morgan

PHOTOGRAPHS by Alamy Stock Photo/Sean Chinn @ greatwhitesean, cover, Shane Gross, 9; Dreamstime/ Alexandre Dionne, 8, Wksp, 4; Getty Images/Jana Kriz, 5; Shutterstock/Benny Marty, 2-3, Bohbeh, 13, Ciril Monteiro, 10-11, Eric Isselee, 14, frantisekhojdysz, 12, HunterKitty, 11, Jonas Gruhlke, 7, MDay Photography, 6-7

Printed in India